Francisco V. Aguilera, Ramón Céspedes

Notes About Cuba

Slavery. I. African slave trade. II. Abolition of slavery. III. Inferences from

the last presidential message. The revolution. IV. Forces employed by

Spain against Cuba V. Condition of the revolution. VI. Spanish anarchy in

Cuba

Francisco V. Aguilera, Ramón Céspedes

Notes About Cuba

Slavery. I. African slave trade. II. Abolition of slavery. III. Inferences from the last presidential message. The revolution. IV. Forces employed by Spain against Cuba V. Condition of the revolution. VI. Spanish anarchy in Cuba

ISBN/EAN: 9783337125431

Printed in Europe, USA, Canada, Australia, Japan

Cover: Foto ©Andreas Hilbeck / pixelio.de

More available books at **www.hansebooks.com**

NOTES ABOUT CUBA.

SLAVERY.

THE REVOLUTION.

As it appears likely that matters relating to the existence of Slavery in Cuba, and to the War which the Cubans have been waging for three years to throw off the yoke of Spain, may soon be discussed in the Congress of the United States, we deem it proper, under the circumstances, to record the few following facts and statements.

FRANCISCO V. AGUILERA,

RAMON CESPEDES,

Commissioners of the Republic of Cuba.

NEW YORK, *January* 4, 1872.

I

THE AFRICAN SLAVE-TRADE.

On the 24th of September, 1817, the Spanish Government entered into a treaty with that of Great Britain, by which, in consideration of the sum of £400,000, to be paid by Great Britain to Spain, the latter engaged to put a stop, from and after the 30th day of May, 1820, to the traffic of slaves, which its subjects were carrying on from the coast of Africa. Great Britain fulfilled her engagement, but Spain continued to tolerate the importation of slaves into Cuba, although, in order to hush the remonstrances of England, she occasionally issued royal orders, in which the Captains-General were urged to prosecute more severely any clandestine importation of negroes. The Captains-General, thoroughly aware of the spirit of their government, and finding moreover that the illicit traffic was an inexhaustible source of wealth to themselves, took good care not to harass it; on the contrary, they rather encouraged it, as a political measure, trusting that the Cubans would abandon all idea of independence through dread of the negro race.

Among the royal orders issued by Spain at the instance of England, which prove how scandalously the slave-trade was carried on, those only need be cited of the 2d of January, 1826, by which the purchase of Africans is declared a theft, that of the 2d of April, 1832, and that of the 2d of November, 1835.

Under date May 25, 1840, the British Government addressed a note to the government of Spain, with a request that an investigation be made as to all negroes landed in Cuba subsequent to the 30th of October, 1820, and that they be se at liberty. On the 20th of January, 1841, the same demand was repeated, but Spain managed to elude it.

Such open violations of the treaty caused a fresh one to be drawn up between England and Spain, which was settled on the 28th of June, 1835, for the purpose of ending the trade in Africans, and by which Spain engaged to pass a law, within two months after the ratification of the treaty, under which any of her subjects engaging in the trade should be severely punished. Ten years passed before any such law was passed (1845), and the slave-trade meanwhile continued.

The inefficiency of the penal law referred to and the remonstrances of the British Government obliged Spain, in 1865, to pass a new law, apparently more severe than the former, but which, like it, was not enforced ; for the slave-trade flourished up to the breaking out of the Cuban insurrection in 1868, and it was only when the confusion caused by this latter event became general over the island that an impediment was placed to a trade which had been officially condemned by the government of Madrid, but which had always been encouraged by its delegates in Cuba, a convincing proof either of the corruption of the Spanish Government, or of its inability to enforce compliance with its most solemn engagements.

The Cubans have ever been opposed to the traffic in slaves from Africa, and have availed themselves of every possible opportunity to protest against its continuance. Many, from the mere fact of having dared to protest against it, have been summarily exiled as dangerous innovators, and this is one of the best proofs of the deceit of the Spanish Government in the fulfillment of its treaty obligations.

Among many similar addresses to the authorities on the subject, one deserves to be mentioned. It is a representation made under date of 29th of November, 1843, by the leading planters of Havana, and Matanzas, to the Captain-General, in which they say " that it is time that this illicit traffic, the scorn of the civilized world, a hideous abyss in which all hope of security or future welfare was buried, should cease," and in which they request him "inflexibly to prosecute the clandestine traffic in African negroes until he had entirely suppressed it." They made a similar request in February, 1844, and on various subsequent occasions, but no notice was ever taken of them.

A private association was formed in Havana, in November, 1865, by permission of the Captain-General. Its object was to aid the "complete and final suppression of the illicit trade, known as the African slave-trade," and its members bound themselves on their honor "not to acquire possession in any shape, directly or indirectly, from the date of their joining the association, of any African negro landed on the island subsequent to the 19th day of November, 1865." The Spaniards, mostly slave-traders, were alarmed; they accused the associates of being revolutionists, and induced the Captain-General to withdraw the permission he had granted.

Finally the Commissioners from Cuba and Porto Rico, elected by the city councils of those islands, and sent to Madrid to report upon the reforms which their constituents claimed, demanded, on the 29th of January, 1869, that the African slave-trade should be declared *piracy*. They obtained absolutely nothing.

II.

ABOLITION OF SLAVERY.

The Islands of Cuba and Porto Rico furnish probably the only examples of slave-holding colonies spontaneously demanding of the mother country the abolition of slavery.

In the investigation instituted by the Spanish Government, in 1866, to inquire into what reforms those islands required, one of the first propositions of the commissioners who had been elected by the city councils was that slavery should be abolished. The Commissioners from Porto Rico, induced thereto by the small number of slaves on that island and the favorable condition of the country, at once applied for immediate abolition, with or without indemnity. The organization of landed property in Cuba, the large number of slaves on that island, the majority of them Africans smuggled into the country, and sundry other circumstances, prevented the Cuban commissioners from being as radical as their colleagues from Porto Rico; but they nevertheless submitted a plan by which slavery would be abolished in thirteen years, with indemnity to the owners, and without any heavy tax upon the people. Both plans met with the most determined opposition from the persons selected directly by the government to assist in the investigation. Most of these persons were natives of Spain, but had been government employees in Cuba, where many of them had grown rich by means of the slave-trade. Of course the government turned as deaf an ear to the proposals for abolition as it did to all other proposals for reform, economic, administrative and political, made by the commissioners from the Antilles.

At that time, scarcely any one in Spain spoke at all of abolition ; on the contrary, the general opinion among politicians was that the institution of slavery was indispensable in the Antilles, in order to keep them dependent on the mother country. It was only after the revolution of September, 1868, that the abolition propaganda arose, and it owes its origin rather to a desire to appear to European nations consistent with the radical principles enunciated in that revolution, than to any deep conviction, or to any fixed determination to carry out its tenets. The best proof of this is that when Sor. Moret, one of the new and most enthusiastic abolitionists, became Colonial Minister, he thought that he had appeased his conscience by the law which was approved by the Cortes, on the 23d of June, 1870.

The pith of said law consists in declaring free only,

1. Those born after the publication of the law. (Art. I.)

2. Those who have served in the Spanish army, and those who have assisted the troops during the present insurrection. (Art. III.)

3. Those who at the date of the publication of the law may have attained the age of 60 years, and others when they attain it. (Art. IV.)

4. The slaves of the Government and those known as *emancipados*. (Art. V.)

5. Those who have been cruelly punished, when their owners are punished by law for the offense. (Art. XVII.)

6. Those who are not registered as slaves in the census, to be taken on the 31st of December, 1870. (Art. XIX.)

Those freed under the 1st article are to remain under the care of the owner of the mother. (Art. V.) The patron shall have the benefit of the labor of the slave, so freed, without compensation, up to the age of eighteen years. (Art. VII.) On the arrival of the freedman at that age, he shall earn one-half of the wages of a free man, according to his class and trade. Of wages so earned, one-half shall be paid to him, and the other retained to form a capital for him, as hereinafter provided. (Art. VIII.) And when the freedman shall attain the age of twenty-two years, he shall enter into the enjoyment of all his rights, and his capital be handed to him.

Slaves over sixty years of age may remain in the houses of their owners, the latter thereby acquiring the character of patron, but not being obliged to pay for any labor performed by them. (Art. XIV.)

By article XXI., flogging is suppressed, as also the selling of children under fourteen years of age away from their mothers, or of either member of a married couple apart from the other.

By article XX., the Government engages to issue an ordinance for the fulfillment of the law ; and by Article XXI., to present to the Cortes, *as soon as the deputies from Cuba have been admitted thereto*, a bill for the emancipation, with indemnity, of such as may continue in slavery after the execution of this law.

According to this law then, the only slaves who are emancipated at once are the *"emancipados,"** who are so already, although the government keeps them in a state of real slavery, the slaves belonging to the State, who are very few, and the useless ones of over sixty years of age ; for such as are born in Cuba after the publication of the law remain slaves up to the age of twenty-two, and may meanwhile be transferred from one patron or holder to another, as if they were real slaves. (Art. XI.) Moreover, the greater number, if not all of those born some months after the publication of the law, will certainly appear, when opportunity arises for its application, with antedated certificates of baptism, and consequently remain absolute slaves all their lives.

The same may be said of such slaves, over sixty years old, as, on account either of their strength or skill, their owners may wish to keep ; for any convenient age may be easily assigned to these slaves, without its being in the power of many of the

---

* The Spanish Government in Cuba calls, by antiphrasis, negroes from Africa, the scandalous manner of whose landing has been made the subject of judicial proceedings, *emancipados.* These negroes should be free, in accordance with the treaty with England, but Spain has always kept them in absolute slavery,both the government and its employees profiting from their labor.   Frequently, these emancipados are sold as regular slaves, the owner merely changing their names.

latter, on account of their having been imported from Africa, to prove their real age.

Not less deceptive is the clause which apparently suppresses flogging. (Art. XXI.) The law does not prohibit it, nor does it impose any penalty for any one who shall exercise it upon his slaves or upon those under his charge, only in Article IX., which relates to causes which end a guardianship, it mentions "the abuses of the patron in *punishments ;*" which proves that punishment can be applied discretionally ; and as the laws relative to slavery, now in force in Cuba, allow an owner to inflict up to twenty-five lashes at one time upon a slave, it is fair to infer that as long as the number of lashes inflicted does not exceed that number, the owner will incur no risk of being punished for abuse or cruelty, especially when the judges who might condemn him are of his own race, and probably slave-owners themselves.

But so many and such skillfully devised restrictions upon freedom have not, however, appeared to the Spanish Government sufficient to induce it to put its own plan in execution. The law of abolition is a dead-letter in Cuba, notwithstanding the publication of it by the Captain-General in the *Gaceta* of Havana on the 28th of September, 1870, for its execution, and notwithstanding all the assertions made to the American Minister in Madrid by the Ministers of Spain. By Article XX. of the law, the Government was bound to issue a special ordinance for its execution ; but as it has issued no such ordinance, although a year and a-half have transpired since the passage of the law, it is of course inoperative; not even has the census of the slaves, been taken which ought to have been taken on the 31st of December, 1870. And so certain is it that the law is not carried into effect in Cuba, that the member from Asturias, Sor. Labra, during the session of the Cortes of the 10th of July last, called the Colonial Minister to account for the non-fulfillment of the law, after its publication. A month later, on the 16th of August, the Abolitionist Society of Madrid presented an address to the Colonial Minister, published in the papers of that city, in which he was requested to order the fulfillment of this preparatory law of abolition, and in which were cited sundry cases which proved that, in Cuba, no notice was taken of the law. The law provides (Art. XXI.) that when mothers are sold, their children under fourteen years old shall not be separated; nevertheless, the Havana papers are full of advertisements in which violations of this rule are publicly proposed. The Abolition Society copies, in its address, as a sample among many others, the following: "For sale, *together or apart*, a negress, washer, ironer and cook; has one daughter twelve years old, another seven, and a son eleven years old." We might quote a number of similar advertisements of more recent date. We will limit ourselves to translating two selected at random from the *Diario de la Marina* of November 28 and of December 1: "For sale, a negress; delivered ten days ago; a good washer, ironer and hairdresser; has a good and abundant supply of milk; *without the child.*" "For sale, a negress; excellent washer and ironer, young; and has a daughter three years old; for $600; the daughter for 15 ounces ($255)." In the first case, the mother is offered for sale apart from her new-born child; in both cases, two girls, born after the publication of the law on the 28th of September, 1870, and who consequently should be free, are offered for sale as slaves. Can any further proof be wanted of the shamelessness with which Spain violates her most solemn obligations, and laughs at the opinion of civilized nations, passing laws apparently humane without any intention of enforcing them?

How different has been the conduct observed by the Cuban patriots! The 24th article of their constitution declares that "all the inhabitants of the Republic of Cuba are absolutely free," and it is a matter of fact that there is not a single slave in the territory where their arms and their banner have penetrated.

III.

INFERENCES DRAWN FROM PRESIDENT GRANT'S MESSAGE.

The article of the Cuban constitution, just quoted, proves how convinced the Cubans are of the intimate connection existing between abolition of slavery and the independence and welfare of their country. Taught by the history of the United States, they have determined not to leave to chance the solution of a problem which, in the course of time, might imperil the very existence of their republic; and foreseeing greater evils, they have, in the very act of their constitution, recognized the equality of all the races which compose her population, trusting thereby to destroy, at the start, all ele- ments that might cause dangerous perturbations further on. When their enemy, the Spaniard, is conquered, everybody in Cuba will be a citizen in the enjoyment of equal rights, irrespective of his or her previous condition, or of the race to which he or she may belong.

The Government of the United States has, perhaps, at last, turned its attention to this article of the Cuban Constitu- tion, and comparing it with the hypocrisy with which Spain has always laughed at her promises of abolition, has under- stood the duties which their antecedents, their position in America, and their representation among the civilized nations of the world impose upon them. Possibly this is the meaning of the paragraph of the last presidential message, in which President Grant, after reproaching Spain for the non-fulfillment of the offers she voluntarily made on the subject of the Antilles, and for not enforcing her laws, apparently framed for the abolition of slavery in Cuba and Porto Rico, recommends Congress to enact laws which shall prevent American citizens from possessing, directly or indirectly, slave property abroad. Possibly, this Great Republic, regenerated in its social condition, and comprehending that a Holy Mission has fallen to its lot, has resolved to play the same noble part with regard to slavery that England played with regard to the slave-trade. Might not the United States, by exterminating slavery on this continent, earn as imperishable glory as England earned by the suppression of the slave-trade? Even England appears so to have regarded this matter, for (see letter from Mr. Sickles to Mr. Fish, Dec. 29, 1869) she has expressed her willingness to *second any suggestions* emanating from the United States on the subject of slavery in Cuba and Porto Rico, thus ceding the place of honor to which she is justly entitled in this work of redemption.

Although at first sight they may not appear so, these suggestions of the President, if consonant with the precedents of a great nation, which has just emerged from a violent convulsion which resulted in the freedom of four millions of human beings, must be foreshadowings of a humanitary policy. If it be just to prevent an American citizen from holding slave property in Cuba, or from being interested, directly or indirectly, in slaves; if this citizen is not to expect his government to exercise its power for his protection in the enjoyment of such prohibited property, it is just that the position thereby assumed by the United States should aim, through the inevitable loss to the master, at the amelioration of the condition of the slave. In case, for instance, that the Spanish Government had, either by embargo or confiscation, seized slaves owned by an American citizen, would the government of Washington consent that these slaves should be retained in a state of servitude? Will it allow its citizen to be despoiled of his property for the benefit of the spoiler, and not for the emancipation of the slave? We cannot conceive it. The American nation cannot adopt a mean and pharisaic policy on this question.

Any law imposed by their own government on American

citizens which would prevent them from holding slaves abroad, and any refusal of this Government to protect such citizens in the holding of such prohibited property, cannot intend to injure them, but merely the elevated and generous object of the redemption of the slave. The rescuing of a slave from an American citizen, for the purpose of placing him in the clutches of the ruling Spaniards, would be morally as unjust an act as can well be imagined, and would be moreover a scandalous connivance at the very evil sought to be remedied.

The government of the United States, while it accepts at the hands of its citizen, in obedience to its laws, the manumission of one or more slaves, must consider itself in duty bound to enforce the transformation of that property, in order that the newly created person may not be robbed of his sacred rights ; and when it defends one of its citizens, whose property may have been embargoed or confiscated, from the tyrannical abuses of the Spanish Government, it may say to him, " You shall own no slave ;" but it will never allow the spoiler to become possessed of such slaves, or to re-rivet their chains forever. In either case, it will inevitably and logically be obliged to insist upon the slave being freed, and to see that the punic faith of Spain, which has caused England so much trouble and expense in the matter of the slave trade, does not by subterfuge and deceit keep such freedman in a state of servitude.

IV

FORCES EMPLOYED BY SPAIN AGAINST CUBA.

The Spanish Government pretends to despise the Cuban revolution, it denounces the patriots as robbers, mostly negroes and Chinamen, wandering in the woods, and always flying before the sight of a Spanish bayonet. Documents, however, which it has at times been obliged to publish, and the indiscretions of the official journals, reveal how false these assertions are, and the great sacrifices which Spain imposes upon herself in order to face this vilified revolution. A few facts suffice to prove this statement:

ARMY.—When the revolution commenced in October, 1868, Spain had an army of 19,700 men of all arms in Cuba, of whom at least 10,000 were fit for active service in the field, leaving 9,700 for the garrisoning of fortresses, jails, hospitals, etc.

From 1st December, 1868, up to 1st December, 1871, over 60,000 soldiers have been landed from Spain, (*Diario de la Marina*, Dec. 6,) or say, 20,000 each year. Lately some more have arrived, and even now it is announced that 30,000 are to be sent to the island, in three divisions, each of which will be commanded by a general officer. To this force must be added nine regiments and some thirty companies of contra-guerillas, which a year ago numbered over twelve thousand men. Besides these the *Volunteers* are scattered through every town on the island, and it may be safely stated that they have never been under forty thousand ; for although on more than one occasion the Havana papers have asserted that they amounted to a hundred thousand, it was only foolish talk, for there has never been in the whole island that number of men capable of bearing arms. Anyway, Spain has always had over thirty thousand regular troops in the field, backed by forty or fifty thousand volunteers, the latter perfectly armed, and fit at any rate to garrison the towns and to prevent any risings in favor of the revolutionary cause, which last eventuality the Spaniards always guarded against by forbidding the creoles to have arms in their possession.

LOSSES.—The losses which the Spanish army in Cuba has suffered are so enormous that the government has never dared to publish an official statement of them. Nevertheless it has been stated in the Madrid papers of 26th of Oct. last, and the government has not denied it, that from the commencement of the war up to February 1, 1871, that is, in less than two years and a half, 29,700 men and 1,748 officers of the regular army had died, or nearly fifty per cent. of the whole number which arrived from the peninsula during that period ; a fact which explains the necessity Spain is under of sending twenty thousand men to Cuba every year, simply to make good the losses.

NAVY.—In 1870, before she received the thirty gunboats built in New York, Spain had in Cuban waters fifty-two (52) vessels of war of all classes, carrying about four hundred (400) guns. We have no reliable data on which to estimate any subsequent increase of either ships or guns; but it is well known that almost the whole fleet of Spain, including her best iron-clads, are employed to-day in watching the coast of Cuba.

ARMAMENT.—From the 1st of November, 1868, to the middle of December, 1871, the Spaniards have imported into Cuba from New York the following arms :

FOR THE ARMY AND VOLUNTEERS.

Remington rifles,	40,281
Peabody rifles,	5,501
Peabody carbines,	1,875
	47,657

2

CONSIGNED TO THE ARTILLERY DEPARTMENT FOR VOLUNTEERS.

Remington rifles, ...	19,718
Peabody rifles, ...	4,451
Remington carbines, (for cavalry,) .	6,629
Peabody carbines, (for cavalry,) . .	4,062
Carbines of other patterns, . .	46
Muskets of other patterns, . .	641
Pistols and revolvers of various patterns	562
	83,766

FIRE ARMS OF VARIOUS PATTERNS, IMPORTED BY CORPORATIONS, VOLUNTEERS, AND PRIVATE PERSONS.

From the United States, . . .	5,000
From Spain, ...	3,500
Total, ...	92,266

The *Diario de la Marina*, the official paper of Havana, of December 2, 1871, from which we take the foregoing statement, calculates the cost of the arms at $1,450,000.

EXPENSES OF THE WAR.—The *Diario de la Marina* of November 14, 1871, published an *authentic* statement of the expenses caused by the war from November 14, 1868, to the end of October, 1871. They amount to $70,339,658 40, or $23,446,532 80 for each of the three years. It must be borne in mind, that, in this amount, the contributions, ironically termed voluntary, but which are really forced ones, and which are frequently exacted from the people for the support of the volunteers, are not included; neither, we believe, is the interest on the debt due by the Government to the Spanish Bank of Havana, nor the amount due to the Steamship Company of Antonio Lopez & Co., for transportation of troops. Were these items added, the expenses of the war would be increased by three to four millions of dollars a year. The amount confessed, $23,446,532 80, suffices, however, to prove that Spain requires twenty thousand fresh men each year wherewith to prosecute the war, and that each man costs her $1,172 32 per annum, and that she sacrifices every day fifty-five of her sons in an inglorious and hopeless war.

It might be thought that, as the revolution, according to

Spanish assertions, is on its last legs, the expenses of the war, for the present year, would be considerably diminished. Let us see if the Spanish Government shares this belief.

In the general budget for the Island of Cuba, for the fiscal year 1871–72, presented to the Cortes by the Colonial Minister on the 26th of October last, the income is calculated at $40,091,833 80, and the expenditure at $27,481,570 57, showing, consequently, a net revenue of $12,610,263. In this statement the ordinary expenses of the army and navy figure for $11,978,878, and the extraordinary ones only for $705,385. But the Minister states that the $12,610,263 net revenue will likewise be applied to this purpose; so that, in reality, the army and navy expenses for the present campaign are estimated at $25,294,526, or at $1,747,994 more than each of the preceding ones. And even this amount will not suffice; for the Colonial Minister publicly declares that the surplus of income over expenditure will not suffice to *cover the deficits of former years*, and to attend to *the extraordinary expenses of the war*, on which accounts he requests the Cortes to authorize him " to establish (*discretionally and without consulting the Cuban people*) such duties and taxes as the necessities of the war may require, and to use credit for raising money for the treasury of Cuba."

A ministerial crisis caused the suspension of the Cortes before the Budget was approved ; but this approval is a mere matter of form ; and the fact of his not having obtained it would in nowise prevent the Minister from exacting the contributions exactly as if the Budget had been approved. The Cortes have never failed to give the Executive *carte-blanche* in all matters relative to the oppression of the colonies, and in the very debate, which resulted in the closing of the Cortes, all parties unanimously recognized how dangerous the Cuban revolution was for the integrity of the nation, and agreed that the sacrifices for its suppression should be illimited.

Finally, even King Amadeus, although not as yet very firmly seated on his throne, has expressed a desire to come in person to Cuba, in order to finish the insurrection ; and although he has since, under wiser advice, determined not to run such a risk, he has, unless the telegraph lies, taken the trouble to go from Madrid to Santander for the sole purpose of addressing 800 soldiers who were about to sail for Havana.

And all this—for the persecution of a few vagabonds roaming about in the woods!

V.

CONDITION OF THE REVOLUTION.

The Spanish Government and its agents unceasingly repeat, day by day, and in every conceivable manner, that the insurrection is dying out, and they have even had the *Té Deum* chanted in their churches, in thanks to the Almighty for the pacification of the island. Notwithstanding these unwearied assertions, Spain continues to forward troops to Cuba ; court-martials and the volunteers continue their work of assassinating, exiling and confiscating *en masse*, and the papers of Havana are filled with accounts of engagements between the insurgents and the Spanish troops, proving the anarchy of the country, and the fact that the war is being waged in the same spirit of ferocity with which Spain first commenced it.

The Republican institutions of Cuba Libre, notwithstanding all the contrary statements made by its enemies, continue to rule, as regularly as can be expected in an island blockaded by the superior forces of its opponents, who commit everything to fire and sword. As when, ten years ago, the United States Government offered Spain its good services for the termination of the conflict with the recognition of the independence of the island, so, to-day, the Cubans hold their own from Santiago de Cuba to the district of the Five Cities, and if they are unable to record any decisive victories, the fault is due solely to the difficulties they experience in receiving arms and ammunition from abroad, whilst their enemy enjoys every possible facility for obtaining them.

In confirmation of the foregoing facts we subjoin solely a statement of the armed bodies which, a short time ago, composed the patriot army, omitting from such statement those who, for the want of arms, are unable to join the ranks; and a short report of some of the engagements which have taken place during the last few months. The statement of the Cuban army has been formulated from the last official dispatches received from the Cuban Government, and in the compilation of the engagements, we have made use only of the official dispatches of the Cuban commanding officers and the advices published in the Spanish papers of Havana. In both cases, we have carefully endeavored to avoid all exaggeration.

The liberating army is composed of three army corps, named the army of Oriente (the East), the army of Camaguey, and the army of Las Villas. These three army corps comprise all the organized forces of the Republic, and number, as per last advices received from the Cuban Government together over ten thousand well-armed, drilled and equipped soldiers. Besides these there are in the territory occupied by the patriot forces numberless small bands of men who hostilize detached bodies of Spaniards, whenever an opportunity occurs, but who, for want of firearms, are not incorporated in the organized regiments of the army.

ARMY CORPS OF ORIENTE.

Commander-in-Chief, General Modesto Diaz.

Division of Santiago de Cuba, Major-Gen. Commanding, Maximo Gomez.

Regt's.	Commander.	Localities.	No. of Men.
1 and 2	Col. Jesus Perez.	Cobre.	600
3	Lt. Col. Prado.	Baracoa.	450
4	Lt. Col. Guillermo Moncada.	Baracoa.	550
5	Lt. Col. Pacheco.	Guantanamo.	450
6	Brig. Calisto Garcia.	Jguani.	600
		Total,	2,650

Division of Holguin, Gen. Commanding Jose Inclan.

Regt's.	Commander.	Localities.	No. of Men.
1	Col. Fco. Herrero.	West.	300
2	Gen. Inclan.	East.	500
		Total,	800

Division of Bayamo, Gen. Commanding, Luis Figueredo.

Regt's.	Commander.	Localities.	No. of Men.
1	Maj.-Gen. N. Garrido.	Manzanillo.	550
2	Gen. Luis Figueredo.	Bayamo.	450

Total, . . . 1,000

Grand Total Army Corps of Oriente, . . . 4,300

ARMY CORPS OF CAMAGUEY.

Commander-in-Chief, Gen. Vicente Garcia.

Division of Las Tunas, General Commanding, Vicente Garcia.

Regt's.	Commander.	Localities.	No. of Men.
1	Gen. Vicente Garcia.	Santa Rita.	650
2	Brig. Francisco Vega.	Arenas.	400

Total, . . . 1,050

Division of Camaguey, Gens. Commanding, Ignacio Agramonte.

Gen. Ignacio Agramonte.

Regt's.	Commander.	Localities.	No. of Men.
1	Lt. Col. La Rosa.	Guaicanamar.	300
2	Col. Agramonte Porro.	"	400
3	Lt. Col. Espinosa.	"	250
4	Lt. Col. Manuel Suarez.	Guimaro.	300
5	Lt. Col. Anto. Rodriguez.	Cubitas.	200

Total, . . . 1,450

Grand Total Army Corps of Camaguey . . . 2,600

ARMY CORPS OF LAS VILLAS.

Commander-in-Chief, Major Gen. Mateo Casanova.

				No. of Men.
Division of Trinidad,	Gen. Com. Brig. Juan Villegas,			700
Division of Santi Espiritu,	" " Brig. Jose Villamil,			800
Division of Villa Clara,	" " Brig. Carlos Ruloff,			600
Division of Cienfuegos,	" " " Juan Villegas,			700
Division of Remedios,	" " " Salome Hernandez,			600

Grand Total Army Corps of Las Villas 3,400

RECAPITULATION.

Army corps of Oriente, ... 4,300
Army corps of Camaguey, ... 2,600
Army corps of Las Villas, ... 3,400

Grand Total, . . 10,300

The following reports are compiled from the latest official documents received from the Government of Cuba, which extend up to the end of September last. Since that date various important engagements have occurred between the forces of the Liberating army and those of the Spaniards, but no mention is made of them under this head, because the official reports of them have not as yet been received. It must be borne in mind that the nature of the war waged by the Cubans for their liberation from the tyrannical yoke of Spain, is chiefly of a guerilla character. In consequence of the inferior number of their armed and organized soldiery in comparison with that of their enemy, they studiously avoid the possibility of being overwhelmed by superior numbers in the open field ; and that they are enabled to carry out their system, is best evidenced by the inability of the Spaniards to record any important victories. Again, the Cubans, owing to the difficulty of obtaining it from abroad, are as yet unprovided with artillery, on which account, whenever they capture a town or city, as they captured Las Tunas, Jguani, Baracoa and others, they sack and destroy it, and retire without attempting to hold it.

The following reports, therefore, selected at random from the official reports of various commanders in different portions of the territory occupied by the Cubans, extending over fully two-thirds of the Island, will contain accounts of no pitched battles and of no decisive victories, but if taken as specimens of what is occurring every day and every night in every part of the Eastern and Central Departments, will give the reader an idea of the activity of the Cubans, and of the slow but certain manner by which they are, little by little, destroying the enemies of their country and insuring its independence.

Spanish accounts, derived from the Havana papers and extending to the end of November last, will be found further on, under a separate head.

*Operations of the Liberating Army in Cuba, up to the Last
Received Official Advices.*

June, 1871.—Gen. Maximo Gomez ordered the 4th, 5th
and 6th regiments of his division to take possession of the line
between the jurisdiction of Santiago de Cuba and Guantanamo. The column had scarcely encamped on the " Loma de
la Galleta," when it was attacked by a numerous body of the
enemy. The engagement lasted four hours, and although the
Spaniards were reinforced during the action by a large force
of contra-guerillas, they were finally repulsed. In their retreat they were harassed by the Cubans, in whose hands they
left their killed and wounded. They fell back to their entrenched camp at Santa Rita. In this action the Spaniards
lost 89 men, 24 horses, 35 Remington rifles, besides a quantity
of clothing, shoes and ammunition.

On the 13th of the same month, the Spaniards renewed the
attack with a force of over 1500 men, losing 11 killed, many
wounded, and 13 taken prisoners. The Cubans on this occasion captured 6 Peabody rifles and some ammunition.

On the 17th a body of 300 Cubans advanced close to the
city of Santiago de Cuba, meeting only with 25 volunteers,
whom they captured. During this march 18 Cubans joined
the column.

August. On the 4th, the Cubans, under Gen. Gomez, attacked and captured the strongly fortified Spanish camp on
the estate La Indiana, in the jurisdiction of Guantanamo. It
was obstinately defended, and of the 40 men who composed
its garrison, five only escaped. After overcoming this first
obstacle, the Cubans overran the whole jurisdiction of Guantanamo, and captured and destroyed fourteen of the best coffee estates in the district of Monte Ruz. The Spaniards made
no appearance until the 8th of August, when they made a re-
connaisance in force at the headquarters of Gen. Gomez,
situated at El Macio. The enemy retired after a short and
quick fire, in which they lost several men. " Later on," Gen.
Gomez writes, " on the 11th, 13th, 15th, 23d and 24th, we

were vigorously attacked, but the enemy gained no advantage over us, for although after the last attack, in which they engaged us with over a thousand men and six pieces of artillery, under command of General Palanca, Governor of Santiago de Cuba, they managed to enter our camp, which was hardly defensible, they lost an enormous number of men in killed and wounded. This is proved by the vast number of graves that they left, and the many litters they carried away in their retreat. This they effected rather precipitately on the 25th, under the fire of part of my forces, which I had posted advantageously for the purpose. On our side we had thirty-five casualties, of whom five killed and the rest wounded. On the 21st inst., the 5th regiment under Lt.-Col. Moncada, returned and reported to me. On his excursion he had advanced close to the capital (Santiago) and had destroyed various estates, and the store at Guayabal, which was strongly intrenched and garrisoned by twenty-five volunteers, who fled at the approach of his men. With the exception of a few unimportant skirmishes, Col. Moncada reports that he was not harassed by the enemy until the day previous to his return to headquarters, when he met a heavy column on its way to attack my headquarters. He fought them for two hours, routed them, and thus broke up their plan for a combined attack. He lost two killed and three wounded. On the 13th, Col. Prado, in command of the 3d Reg., invaded by my orders, the district of Sagua de Tanamo. He took and destroyed the fortified camp of Miguel, garrisoned by from 30 to 40 men, who fled, as usual. He also captured other intrenchments in that vicinity, all of which, he reports, were feebly defended, and he drove off all the cattle of the district. He possessed himself, moreover, of a large quantity of stored tobacco."

Perhaps nothing will give a better insight into the state of the revolution and the manner of warfare, as waged both by Cubans and Spaniards, than the following despatch of Col. MANUEL CALVAR, operating in the sub-district of Manzanillo, Department of the East, which we copy textually :

"July 3. Lt.-Col. Francisco Guevara reports as follows : The enemy, about 300 strong, appeared in front of my camp at La Sabana del Estribo. I at once ordered a weak fire to be opened upon them, and abandoned the camp. This I did on account of the very short supply of ammunition I then had, although our position was an advantageous one. · Nevertheless, I learn from trustworthy sources from the Spanish camp at Veguita, that my men killed five of the enemy and wounded about forty others. The arms of the wounded, among whom was the traitor Pedro Popa, were carried off on four horses heavily loaded. I had one wounded. On the retreat of the Spaniards they fell in with Major David Baldoquin, his servant and Benigno Baldoquin, who were on a visit at my camp. The Spaniards fired on these three men, wounded and captured Major Baldoquin and took him to Bayamo, where, in spite of his wound and the then weak state of his health, they executed him on arrival.

"July 8. The same Lt.-Col. Guevara, writes: Having again taken possession of my camp at Estribo, I was informed by my rangers, about eight A. M., that the enemy was advancing by the path leading to Rangel. I ordered Captain Margarito Diaz out to meet them with his company. Firing commenced at once, and lasted about one hour. The enemy retired, crossing through the woods behind the Estribo, coming out at Los Toros. They lost fifty-three men killed and wounded. Our casualties were two, my son Francisco Guevara slightly wounded, and one soldier, Joaquin Milanés, killed.

"Same date. Major Emilio Noguera reports : Second Lt. Tomas Mariño with his men approached and fired into the Spanish camp and village of Veguita, on the night of the 4th. He was answered by a very well-sustained fire from the enemy, whom he kept under arms the whole night. The same report of Lt. Mariño, says : Continuing my operations on the 5th, I marched with my fifty men towards the village of Datil, and found the country along the road completely uninhabited, until I arrived within a mile of the village. Close up to the village I fell in with a number of women gathering fruit, who told that the hunger they suffered within the enemy's lines was extreme. I also surprised fifteen men and a lot of children, who, although they were with the Spaniards, I soon learned were not our enemies. The Spaniards had made them believe that the war was ended, and that we kill every body that comes over to our side. So in order to convince them that their fears, and those of other ill-informed persons like them, were groundless, and to disprove the lies of the Spaniards, I left them at liberty, only taking their machetes. On the 6th, I marched towards Jucaibama, and posted myself along the road between that place and Jucaibamita, with my same fifty men. After waiting about one hour, at 10 A.M., a great noise advised me of the approach of the enemy. They were about 150 strong, all on horseback, and with them were some merchants on their way into Manzanillo. I opened fire upon them, and instead of returning it, they ran, never stopping in their flight until they reached the plain of Jucaibamita. Here, being pursued by my men, they halted and faced us. The firing was kept up for over an hour, when they retreated, carrying their wounded with them, the number of whom, to judge from the many streams of blood on the field, must have been very considerable. We did not lose a man.

"July 25. Major Dominguez reports to me, that, being encamped on the estate 'La Caridad,' he sacked the sugar estate Las Ovas, which is distant only half a mile from the Spanish camp on the sugar estate Esperanza; that on the same night he captured nine yoke of oxen from the cattle estate of the traitor, Tomas Ramirez, which he burned to the ground. He also, on the same night, burned the estate of Antonio Lastres. The enemy, although close at hand, did not attempt to interfere.

"July 29. Major Emilio Noguera reports that having, on that day, conveniently posted his men on the main road to Bayamo, he fought forty of the enemy who were proceeding along it, and who fled at the first fire, leaving in our hands eleven horses, a lot of blankets, hammocks, and other effects. The same major fought on the 29th a body of fifty of the enemy, who were driving cattle towards 'El Humilladero,' and who fled at the first discharge, abandoning the cattle, and an officer, who was wounded. Besides this prisoner, who was captured with his Remington, 100 cartridges, a new saddle, and two saddle-bags filled with clothes, there fell into our hands ten horses, with their equipments, a lot of hammocks, blankets, and other effects.

"July 30th. Major Mariano Dominguez reports: I was in my camp at La Caridad with a force composed of the companies Luz de Yara, the company of Capt. José Torres, the company of Capt. Nicolas Garcia, and the one of Capt. Manuel Tamayo; the latter belonging to the division of Bayamo, and the former to that of Manzanillo. I attacked a Spanish body of over a hundred men, who were posted on the estate San Antonio. After half an hour's firing, I dislodged them from their intrenchments, and drove them into a wood, on which I advanced and drove them from it into an opening close by, out of which they fled in disorder. We captured the bugler with his rifle, two other Remingtons, 350 cartridges, seven horses and one mule, besides twenty-seven hammocks, the same number of blankets, and other effects. The Spaniards left one killed. The captured bugler states that we caused them a loss of seventeen, and that they threw away many rifles which I have not yet been enabled to find. We had one killed and two wounded. On the night of the same day, I was attacked by a very heavy body of Spaniards, and determined, in view of the inequality of numbers to withdraw, which I effected without any loss, and after killing three of the enemy.

"August 7. The same Major Dominguez reports: Considering the enemy's camp at La Sal to be weak, I determined to attack it on the night of the 5th. I advanced with the seventy men of my command deployed as skirmishers. A guerilla body of the enemy endeavored to impede them, but were soon dispersed; and then, while drawing a heavy fire from the block-house, at the same time preventing the enemy from leaving his intrenchments, I entered the village and burned a hundred and fifty houses and five stores. On account of the small number of my force, I could not avail myself of the contents of these stores. I captured one flag, one carbine, and twenty cartridges, and killed four of the enemy, without any loss on our side.

"On the 6th inst., while in my camp at Guanal, and having then a hundred and fifty men in my command, I learned by my rangers, that a body of between four and five hundred

Spaniards was at Dulce Nombre, and that they were on the road to my camp. I instructed Majors Dominguez and Noguera to attack them in front, and that Lieut.-Colonel Guevara should operate on their right flank. As soon as these movements were carried out, I opened such a hot fire upon the enemy that, after an hour's firing, they were obliged to retire very hastily. They carried off over fifty killed and wounded; among the former, the colonel in command of the force, (who was killed by Capt. Manuel Sacramento Rodriguez,) and two captains. On our side, we had two killed and seven slightly wounded.

" August 10. Major Emilio Noguera reports under this date : I attacked the enemy's camp at Santa Isabel, close to the city of Bayamo, with the companies ' Estrella,' ' Victoria,' and ' Voluntaria.' I allowed my men to fire only once, and then attacked with the machete, and with such energy, that the enemy was unable to fire more than a few shots. The camp was taken and the place burned to the ground. The enemy left in it twenty-six volunteers killed by the machete, besides the commander of the camp, who was taken prisoner. We captured, besides, twenty-five fire-arms, and a number of machetes and other effects. On our side, only two wounded.

" August 13th. While on the Sotolongo road, in the savannah of La Caridad, with only thirty-five men of my force, I fell in with a body of the enemy consisting of 150 infantry and 110 cavalry. The latter opened fire and retreated under the accuracy of our aim. The infantry then advanced, and, after a quarter of an hour's sharp fighting, fell back upon the cavalry, when the two forces withdrew. The enemy left on the field several dead horses, and carried off eleven men, either killed or wounded. On our side our wounded were the chief of the brigade, who subscribes, and four others, and we lost one killed. During this fight both the officers and men behaved with great coolness and valor, Captain Nicolas Garcia especially distinguishing himself.

"August 23. Major Joaquin Calañas, chief of operations in Guá, reports, under date of 1st September, as follows : On August 23, in the afternoon, a shout from my advanced guard announced the approach of the enemy. We went out to meet them in the savannah of Jó, and opened fire upon them. Notwithstanding their very superior numbers, they retired, after a quarter of an hour's firing, carrying off seven wounded and leaving two dead upon the field. On our side we had only one wounded, the gallant Lieut. N. Rosillo. His rifle was completely ruined by a musket ball.

"August 24. Major Villanueva, accompanied by Capt. Ramon Hernandez Rios, with a force of fifty men, was on the road to Jibacoa, when he found traces of the enemy's having crossed the road in the direction of Las Sierras. He followed them and came up with them at Malangas, where they were about breakfasting upon nothing but rice and the salted beef of the country. This they abandoned, after a short fight, although they numbered over 250. They left eight dead on the ground, while we had not one even wounded.

"September 3. Major Emilio Noguera, on this date, reports that on the 1st he learned from his spies of the approach of a convoy, guarded by a contra-guerilla of thirty men. On the 2d, he posted himself, with forty of his men, which force he divided with Capt. Arcolea, in spots where the convoy must pass. When it reached the place, he poured in only one discharge, and then attacked with the machete. The enemy abandoned the three carts; six volunteers and one Spanish soldier were killed and two were taken prisoners, of whom one was a standard-bearer. Major Noguera captured ten carbines, six cartouch-boxes filled, six machetes, one horse and its equipments, and twelve yoke of oxen. The foregoing is a copy of the original documents.

"Head-Quarters, Sept. 15, 1871.

"MANUEL CALVAR,

"*Col. Chief of Operations.*"

EASTERN DEPARTMENT.

September 18. At one A.M. of the 18th, Gen. Calixto Garcia attacked the town of Iguani with three regiments, divided into six operating bodies. The town was defended by a numerous garrison, which had been, moreover, reinforced the day previous by two hundred men from Manzanillo. The attack lasted over two hours, and the Cubans managed to gain possession of the greater portion of the town. As Gen. Garcia had not intended to remain in the place, he retired in good order, after killing over two hundred of the enemy, and burning the greater portion of the town. He captured a large number of rifles and a rich booty, which consisted largely of the convoy which the enemy had received the day previous, and which was guarded by the two hundred troops which constituted the reinforcement of the place.

During the same day, the Spaniards were further reinforced, from their camps in the neighborhood, by over six hundred men, and attacked the patriots at a place called Palmarito. They were repulsed with heavy loss. The Cubans lost two killed, among whom one major. The above facts are proved by the official dispatch of Gen. Garcia.

The following statements and reports are compiled from the Spanish papers of Havana and other cities, and require no comments:

August.—The *Diario de la Marina* says that Gen. Velasco met with a desperate resistance from the Cuban forces under Gen. Vicente Garcia, and acknowledges the loss of two officers.

September 2.—"During the latter part of August, several engagements took place in the districts of Bagá and Manzanillo."

September 10.—Several engagements in Caunao, Ciego de Avila, and in the mountains of La Pimienta, jurisdiction of Sancti Espiritu.

September 10.—*El Imparcial* of Trinidad says that the insurgents were in that vicinity, and had captured five prisoners.

September 24.—A Spanish camp at Banito was attacked by a Cuban column composed of 200 infantry and 60 cavalry.

October 1.—The *Diario de la Marina* of this date says that the following engagements took place during September:

September 17.—El Rincon dela Sierra.
"   " —Caunao, Jurisdiction of Camaguey.
"   " —In mountains of Pedro Alonzo, Jurisdiction of Las Tunas.
"   18.—Pueblo Viejo.
"   " —Roble Mountains.
"   " —Seborucales.
"   21.—Palma's Bridge.
"   " —Camajuani Road.
"   " —Los Posas.
"   " —Honduras.
"   " —Mendez' Cattle Farm.
"   " —Perindingo Mountains.

The Spanish Commander-in-chief of Sancti Espiritu and Moron reports seven engagements from the 19th to the 26th September, with the insurgents, who have passed to the westward of the celebrated *trocha militar.*

The chief of the Central Department also reports several engagements between his troops and the insurgents at Timini, Las Guasimas, Sierra de Najaza, Sierra del Chorillo, Guaimarillo, Sierra de Cubitas and Yaguajay.

Gen. Morales de los Rios had a very severe engagement with the Cubans under Gen. Vicente Garcia.

The Commander-in-chief of Holguin and Los Tunas reports an engagement with the patriots (September 16) between San Juan de la Puerta and Raja. September 15.—The Cubans attacked the Spanish Camp at Monte Libano, jurisdiction Guantanamo, and took three prisoners. From the 15th to the 19th September, the Cuban Col. Borrero was attacked three times by the Spaniards, between Guantanamo and Tiguabos, in which the Spaniards acknowledge heavy losses. The hamlet of Jobito and four plantations were burned. October (date not stated), Central Department.—Lieut.-Col. Moataner, with a guerilla force of 125 men, had an engagement with the insurgents, in which, according to official despatches, he killed thirteen, and captured a like number of arms, besides destroying the salt-works of Santo Domingo and Las Alegrias, in which there were stored over fifty hundred weight of salt. (*Diario de la Marina*, Nov. 17.) We quote this fact not for its im-

3

portance in a military point of view, but because it goes to prove that the Cubans do not live in the woods like roving beasts, as the Spaniards assert, but that they devote themselves to the industries necessary to life. The official despatches of the Spaniards are filled with accounts of the destruction of cultivated lands, manufactories, tan-yards, etc.

October 15 and 16.—The force of Pedro Castellanos attacked, on two consecutive days, the block-house at Bagá (opposite Nuevitas, Jurisdiction of Camaguey); and although he could not quite get possession of it, one soldier managed to get within the fortification. These forts are defended by artillery and ditches. Castellanos' force comprised 50 to 60 men. (*Diario de la Marina*, November 17.)

October 23.—The columns of San Quintin and Marina, united to others, whose entire number is not stated, under Brig. Campos, attacked the insurgents entrenched in the woods of El Toro. The Spaniards say that the insurgents numbered over one thousand men, of whom six hundred were armed. The result cannot have been very satisfactory for the Spaniards, because they merely state that they fired fifteen cannon shot, and that they took the camp, without mentioning the losses incurred by either side. (*Diario de la Marina*, Nov. 15.)

Nov. 30. The captain of the 6th company of the regiment of Volunteer Rangers of Manzanillo, Don Manuel Ferral y Monge, went out of Guá, in the jurisdiction of Manzanillo, with one hundred and ten men to attack the Cubans who were at a place in the Seirra Maestre, (the high range of mountains on the south coast of Cuba,) called Corral Nuevo. The Cubans received them with a terrible fire, and the Spaniards were forced to retire, with the captain wounded, leaving several dead on the field, besides six whose corpses they carried off. On their retreat the Spaniards were intercepted by another force of Cubans, three times as large as their own, (that is between 300 and 400 men,) under command of Modesto Diaz. From that point the Spaniards continued their retreat to a place where they met a body of reserves of the volunteers of Manzanillo, when the Cubans retreated. The Cubans were well armed. (*Diario de la Marina*, 14 Dec., 1871.)

Nov. (No date stated.) Military district of Holguin and Las Tunas. *Seventy men who were taking the mail* from Majibacoa to San Augustin, met with about two hundred insurgents, and a bloody fight ensued. The Spaniards confess to a loss of seven wounded. (*Diario de la Marina*, Nov. 17.) This is a good proof of the pacification of a country where seventy men are required to convey a letter from one point to another.

We will close this report with extracts of some intercepted letters written by Spaniards in the army, who describe very vividly the efficiency of the system of warfare adopted by the patriots, the discomfiture of our enemies, and the neglect and even cruelty with which Spain treats her own soldiers. The originals of the letters are in our possession.

1.

" COFFEE ESTATE, PROSPERIDAD, *Sept.* 16, 1871.

"*My most esteemed and cherished friend,* — ..... The news from here is that we have plenty of war. On the 1st of August we got a great beating; we had *one hundred and fifty losses,* between killed and wounded, only by the machete and bayonet, and of them (of the insurgents) also plenty killed;— it was fearful;—and nothing more......

"Thy cousin, JUAN GACE."

2.

"*Sept.* 17, 1871.

"*Dear Brother,*—I received yours of May 11, and another letter, of July 13......

"I write to you from a coffee estate, because some of my company came to it in charge of sundry sick and wounded, whom we brought to a provisional hospital which we have on it, and at the same time we came for rations for the column of the provisional military administration which there is in that place. The fact of my not having answered your first, is due to the fact that I have never been in any place from which a letter was likely to reach you; for, during the last three months they have not allowed us one moment's rest,

overrunning the coast from one side to another, because it is
said that the enemy expects a landing of 7000 Yankees, or
Americans, in their favor, with provisions and arms; so that
on the 20th we shall leave here with the convoy to join the
main body. So do not be surprised at any delay in my writ-
ing to you; for do not imagine that this country is as full of
towns as Spain, for there is scarcely one in the whole zone
which we are operating in, and we never go into any except
when we are taking the sick or wounded to the provisional
hospitals; for all that there is, are numbers of sugar and coffee
estates, the greater part of which have been abandoned by
their owners and burned by the enemy. . . . . .

"With respect to the insurrection, it appears to be daily
increasing in extent, and to be adopting a different system of
warfare; for on every side are to be seen small scattered
bodies of from 100 to 300 men; so that almost every day we
have encounters with them. They fire two or three volleys
into us and then run away; and as the woods are very thick
and the ground very broken, we are unable to get up with
them, owing to their better knowledge of the localities. So
that in each ambush which they set for us, they kill ten or
twelve of our men and we scarcely ever hit one, unless it be
in the capture of some camp, and on these occasions they offer
a resistance never equalled. So that, as far as I can judge,
this will never have an end, until we do what we' did in Santo
Domingo and abandon the island to them, notwithstanding
any thing else which the papers may say to deceive the youth
of Spain; for this is the truth of the real character of the
war. It appears now that the king has sent for Valmaseda,
in order that he may inform him of the state of the insurrection; we do not know what result it will produce.

" Among the enemy fresh hands appear every day; but the
greater part are negroes, mulattoes, native Cubans, Chinese
and other colors, and many Spaniards, who are the worst of
all. Whenever firing is commenced, they raise great shouts,
as if they thought to frighten us with their yells, calling us
every injurious epithet. . . . . . Their trumpets are of horn,
like those used in Spain on the railroad. Our dress is composed
of a blouse of linen, pants of the same, a hat of palm leaf, a

cloak, and a bag slung across the shoulder to carry our rations, a cartridge-box with a hundred Remington cartridges, and the bayonet; so that as the roads are impassable for beasts of burden, except in certain districts, we are obliged to carry rations for six or eight days and then go back to the same place for more; so that what with the heat, and the mosquitoes, which devour us in the woods, our heavy load, and lastly, the long distances which they make us march, this may justly be called a human slaughter-house; and this is the reason why the greater part of the people die of sickness.

"The ration in active service consists of six ounces of rice for two men; three of bacon, two biscuits, and a cup of coffee, without anything else. Now and then we steal a bull in a pasturage, and have a little beef, and we make much of it; but cattle are now so scarce that we hardly ever see one, for you must remember that the insurrection has lasted two years, and that everything has been destroyed either by the enemy or by our troops, and then you may realize how completely devastated the island is. This is all I can tell you in a brief space, for it would require a very extended one to describe all the details of the insurrection.

"The climate has not been so far very bad for me, for there are very few of those who came out with me who have not had either the bilious or the yellow fever; but in any case we shall very few of us have a chance of seeing Spain again, unless this thing is finished; for from one day to another our last hour may come, if not from sickness, from the enemy; so that we live only in trust in God, but death is ever before our eyes. . . . . . . One half of the army has served out its time two to three years ago, but nobody is discharged, and probably no one will be discharged until this is over, which will be a long time hence. . . . &c. And so, good bye.

"Your brother, MAURICIO VILIOIA."

3.
"PROSPERIDAD, *September* 18, 1871.

"*My dearest mother*, who art ever in my thoughts. . . .
You must learn, mother, that I have been very ill, so bad that in the middle of my illness, I heard those who were with me

say, 'He is dying: he won't live out the night;' and others I heard say, "Look here, where shall we bury him?' for they saw that I was half gone. But afterwards Divine Providence chose to allow me to recover, though very slowly, and thanks to the good nourishment I took, although I was spending my good quarters which I had kept to send to you, because I know how much you need them; but during the four months that I was in the hospital, not only did I spend the four or five doubloons which I had for you, but in my bad illness I would have spent much more in medicines, and good nourishment, and on those who were around me; but when the three months were up, out of my doubloons I had only sixteen reals (80 cents) left; and during the last days, when I was already well, I suffered more from hunger than any poor beggar, because my reals were all gone. But now, my mother, I find myself re-established from my illness. And know, mother, that in the seven or eight months that we are here, we have not been able to see a single town, though ever so poor a one, where I could get a scrap of paper and a pen, in order to have answered you, and to-day by a great accident I have arrived at this coffee estate, La Prosperidad, where I met with a person who sold me this piece of paper, which I got after all more for God's sake than for my money. During all that time that I have told you of, always in the woods and swamps; some days wet through; other days crossing rivers with the water up to our middle; and others along the roads and in the mud, always passing bad days and bad times, because we never find where to dry our clothes; and as we have none except what we have on our backs, so much the worse. And this is the reason why so many fall ill here; because we go sweating through the woods, and all of a sudden will fall a perfect deluge of rain, and on top of that the sun and a burning heat. . . . It is a long time since I saw a tile roof, for we go through the woods like bandits. . . . Since I left the hospital, they have sent me, with 10 or 12 others, to a coffee estate; and the work that we have to perform is that every day we make up gangs; one day to some coffee estates; another day to others; other days to carry messages; and every day tramping eight, ten, and up to thirteen and fourteen leagues;

and always very wide-awake on account of the enemy, who, if it were not for his treachery, is not worth anything; but when they hit any of our men, it is because they are in ambush in the woods, and they fire a volley into us at close quarters, and escape. . . . .   RAMON TAMBORERO."

4.

"*September* 19, 1871.

"*Dear Brother,*— . . . I should like to send you some money, but it is three years since they have given me "plus" or anything else. [Plus is the name given to extra pay, or gratification sometimes, given to Spanish soldiers in active service.] . . . But, God willing, I shall go soon, and I will take it with me, and we will enjoy it together. . . .

"EMETERIO LOPEZ CORBAL."

VI

SPANISH ANARCHY IN CUBA.

Spanish dominion in Cuba is sustained solely by the force of cohesion inherent in matters which have lasted a long while, and which occasionally remain standing, for some time after they have rotted internally, and after their foundations have been sapped. So complicated was the machinery of tyranny in Cuba, and so perfectly was its population, morally and physically, entangled by it, that its demolition was a work of great difficulty; but when once a popular impetus has been given to the task, the very means employed by the government for the prevention of its destruction, helps to hasten it. Thus we find that the very relentless ferocity with which the Spaniards have, from the commencement, treated the insurgents, has raised the patriotism of the latter to a pitch of desperation, has demoralized Spain's own agents, has alienated from her the sympathies of every civilized nation, and covered herself with infamy. Thus, also, the organization of the volunteers, whereby the government hoped to separate the Spaniards from the Cubans, and which it deemed the sole element of power deserving of its confidence, has become a Prætorian band which to-day exacts obedience to its bloody will, even from the government, and which has set up a most scandalous state of anarchy.

A few facts, among thousands which we could cite, will suffice to prove this anarchical state of things, and the depth of degradation to which both the Spaniards and the government in Cuba have descended. We will be brief, for it is not our desire to horrify our readers by an enumeration of atrocities which is in reality perfectly inexhaustible.

The volunteers, for many months, paraded a dead sparrow through the principal cities of the island. They kept guard over it, sacrilegiously had funeral masses performed over it by the catholic priests, and the sacred hymns chanted in the presence of crowds of civil and military functionaries. In each city or town the volunteers obliged every body to subscribe, however small a sum, as a proof of his or her patriotism. No one has ever known how much was collected. The origin of this sacrilegious farce was, that the Cubans had nicknamed the Spaniards sparrows, because these little birds are imported from Spain.

The volunteers threatened to kill sundry Spanish military officers of high rank, such as Generals Moret, Buceta, Pelaez, Letona, and others, because they thought these officers were not cruel enough in their treatment of the Cubans; and the officers were obliged to escape from the island in foreign vessels.

On the same account they obliged Captain-General Dulce, who had come from Spain as the representative of the new revolutionary government, to abdicate and return to the Peninsula. They obliged Captain-General De Rodas, who was sent out from Madrid purposely to suppress them, to don their uniform, and to mount guard in the balcony of his palace. They stopped his carriage in the streets of Matanzas and made him put on a Catalonian cap; and at last, tired of making him the instrument of their every whim, they suggested to him that it was time for him to leave, a suggestion with which he at once complied.

Count Valmaseda, on the strength of his unparalleled barbarities, which have earned for him a disgracefully notorious place among the exterminators of mankind, was the idol of the volunteers: they expressed a wish that he should replace De Rodas as captain-general of the island, and the government of Madrid at once acquiesced by appointing him.

The *Voz de Cuba*, the organ of the volunteers in Havana, published, on the 14th of June last, an article, which proposed, as the shortest way of winding up the revolution, the formation in that capital of an association, a " common centre, with branches in all the cities of the island, whose object should be to collect money and form a fund, wherewith to pay such rewards as may be offered for the persons or the heads of the chiefs who have earned most renown for their criminal exploits against Spain." The editor of the *Voz de Cuba* approved the idea, and as no project of this nature remains incomplete in Cuba, it may safely be asserted that the association was organized. On the following day, the 15th June, Captain-General Valmaseda, obsequious to the wish of the volunteers, published a proclamation, in which he offered pardon and thanks *to all deserters from the Spanish army* who should bring in their leaders, alive or dead; a present of a sum of money to all such as should give information of the whereabouts of Cuban encampments, and should lead the Spanish troops to surprise them; and a greater reward still to such as should assist in *the capturing of the principal actors in the revolution.*

One journal in Madrid calls another a filibuster; the latter sues the former for contumely and calumny, and the Court fines the calumniator five hundred dollars. The volunteers of Havana are indignant at the sentence of the court; they open a public and *national* subscription to pay not only this fine, but all others that may in future be imposed for the same offence—and, not satisfied with thus openly countenancing and patronizing contumely and calumny, and insulting the law courts of Spain, they publish a document of which they remit numberless copies to Madrid, which closes with these words: " We request the papers of Spain not to relax in their *noble task*, always certain to find in *our purses every indemnity* for any penalties which, by an inconceivable fatuity, may possibly sometimes be imposed upon them." The subscription sums up thousands of dollars, and the Havana papers are filled with lists in which the subscribers vie with each other in heaping the filthiest of epithets, not only on the editor who brought the suit, but on every minister and every liberal member of the Cortes, who has ever uttered a word in favor of the abolition of slavery in Cuba, or who has ever advocated a more conciliatory policy towards that island.

The reply to be sent by the Cortes to the inaugural address of the King, dated 24th of last May, and which was definitively adopted, with little variation, contained the following paragraph : " A fatal legacy of the ancient *regime*, during which passions were fermenting and an explosion prepared, is the civil war which still burns in Cuba; but the Congress of Deputies shares with Your Majesty the hope that it may be speedily and successfully terminated. The firmness of the Government, the patriotism, gallantry, and sufferings of the navy, of the army, and of the volunteers, the military skill of its chiefs, and the constant ardor of the whole nation, will contribute to this end, jointly with the fact that at length the rebels will be persuaded that, when once they have submitted, they will commence to enjoy the liberties which they seek in vain to obtain by force. Its employment (*that of force by the Cubans*) alone interferes with the fulfillment of the promises made by the revolution, and which will doubtless soon, in accordance with the wish of Congress, be completely realized in the other large Spanish Antilla in which peace has not been disturbed, and in which the full enjoyment of political rights and the abolition of slavery will prevent its being disturbed." The volunteers of Havana at once replied to these conciliatory and inoffensive generalities of the Spanish deputies by the most insulting and open defiance ever hurled at the Congress of any nation. The *Voz de Cuba*, the favorite representative of the volunteers, in its issue of June 31st last, devoted its leading article to this matter, and said among other things, " The paragraph of the projected reply of the Cortes which refers to the Antilles, GIVES A PERFECT IDEA OF THE ABJECT DEGRADATION to which—to their own disgrace— many of those men have descended, who make a stepping-stone of politics, for the attainment of the objects of their vile cupidity. . . . We pass over in silence ' the firmness of the Government,'—our readers can form their own opinions on that matter,—and let us see what it says about ' the rebels being at length persuaded that, after submitting, they will enjoy the liberties which they are now in vain endeavoring to obtain by force.' We cannot possibly imagine that this has been written in good faith, nor that whoever wrote it could believe that, by the hypocritical mask with which he covers up so WICKED AND INSULTING AN IDEA, he could deceive those who, ever watchful for the glory of our honor and for the security of the nation, never lose a moment in sounding the alarm, whenever these are threatened. What! Are the nature of these liberties by chance misunderstood? . . . If any party in power, be it the absolutist or the republican, should evince any such tendencies, we should not hesitate to tell them that WE WOULD IN NOWISE ACKNOWLEDGE THEM; and, although we might not, by reason of superior forces opposed to ours, be able to shake off the ominous yoke of our disgrace, we should in silence keep our opinions until the day arrives for throwing in the faces of the guilty, the curse of the country, and for REPELLING FORCE BY FORCE."

In order to understand the full meaning of this insulting declaration, it must be borne in mind that the censorship of the press still obtains in Havana, and that nothing can be published without the permission of the delegate of the Captain-General; and, as it is impossible to believe that either the Captain-General, entrusted with unlimited power, or any public employee would voluntarily authorize the insults, addressed in the above article to the highest powers of the Spanish nation. the coercion, which the volunteers exercise over the highest authorities of Cuba, humiliating them as they choose, is evident.

The above occurred in the short duration of the Ruiz Zorilla radical ministry, when the democratic press of Spain reproached the volunteers of Cuba for their lawlessness, and when it was demanding that the law on slavery should be complied with and that liberal concessions be made to the Cubans. In case, however, the threat of *repelling by force* any laws that were unpleasant to them was not sufficiently clear, the same paper, *Voz de Cuba*, takes pains to make it so, in its editorial article of the 27th of July, in which it asks, " Will the country be resigned enough to submit to this dangerous experiment ?" (The experiment of granting liberal concessions to the Cubans.) "We believe that those who have learned how to overcome by their firmness the dangers which threatened our nationality, will know, when the time comes, how, if only in defense of a principle, to oppose energetically a certain and well defined calamity. And we are convinced that, between a sectarian obsequiousness which is ready to sacrifice everything to a metaphysical and seductive idea, and a resistance in defence of country and civilization, public opinion will absolve them, (the volunteers,) from all FATAL CONSEQUENCES WHICH THE CONFLICT MAY ENTAIL."

About the middle of 1870, Don Nicolas Azcarate came to New York, confidentially authorized by the Spanish Government to offer the Cubans a general amnesty, the disarmament of the volunteers, the return of sequestrated property, and certain liberal institutions, on condition that the insurgents would lay down their arms. The official representatives of Cuba reported to their government the propositions of Spain ; but both these representatives and the leading Cubans who were called together for the consideration of the propositions, openly declared to the Spanish envoy that, as far as they were personally concerned, they rejected them. Meanwhile this envoy, distrustful that his proposals had been sent to President Cespedes, sent to Cuba secretly, and on his own account, Juan Clemente Zenea who, (as Mr. Azcarate has since declared in the Madrid paper, *La Constitution*, of Sept. 18, 1871,) left New York provided with a safe-conduct, in the handwriting of and signed by the Spanish minister in Washington, wherein, " by authority of the GOVERNMENT OF THE REGENT AND IN THE NAME OF HIS HIGHNESS AND THAT OF THE SPANISH NATION, he orders all the military and naval authorities of the Island of Cuba and THE VOLUNTEERS to give free pass to Don Juan Clemente Zenea into and out of any port of the Island of Cuba which he might choose and as he deemed most convenient." Zenea reached Cuba and spoke with President Cespedes, who rejected the proposals of Spain. On leaving the island he was captured by the Spaniards, and, in spite of the safe-conduct, taken to Havana, where he was imprisoned in the Cabaña fortress, under the guard of the volunteers. As soon as this was known in Madrid, (we have this from Mr. Azcarate's own statement,) the Duke de La Torre, then President of the Council of Ministers to King Amadeus, " telegraphed to the authorities of Havana to have the safe-conduct given to Zenea in the name of the Regent of the Kingdom, and of the Supreme Government of the Nation, respected." But the authorities of Havana were powerless under the pressure of the volunteers; and notwithstanding the safe-conduct, notwithstanding the honor of the Spanish nation pledged in that document, and notwithstanding the orders of the Supreme Government transmitted by telegraph, Zenea was shot, after eight months' imprisonment in the ditch of the Cabaña, on the 15th of August. It is to be supposed that the Government of Madrid in defence of its own honor exhausted its efforts to save him.

The atrocities of Carlos Gonzalez Boet, Major of Infantry, reached such a pitch, that the Spanish Government in Cuba even, considered itself obliged to arrest and try him by court martial. The charge brought by a Colonel of Artillery, and which is printed, proved conclusively that Gonzalez Boet had committed various crimes, robberies and murders, by which he was liable to be shot, according to the military code. His victims, however, had been only Cubans, and the Judge Advocate, after enumerating the great services and merit of Boet, asked that he might be condemned merely to six years in the chain gang. The court martial, nevertheless, unconditionally acquitted the accused, and even ordered his pay for the time he was imprisoned to be handed to him at once; and Gonzalez Boet has returned to continue his career of meritorious crimes at the head of the guerillas who helped him to commit them. A letter from Havana, dated July 15, and published in a Madrid paper, endeavours to explain the sentence of the court which acquitted the accused. It states, that on the evening previous to the acquittal, a body of 219 volunteer sergeants waited on the Captain-General Count Valmaseda, and handed him a written document in which they threatened him with a riot in case Boet was not acquitted; and that during the sitting of the court, the room in which it was held was surrounded by mobs of volunteers, yelling, *Viva Boet!*

Don José Dominguez, Captain of Spanish Infantry, was in the village of Veguita, in the jurisdiction of Colon. On Sept. 27, 1870, he ordered a peaceable man to be shot, because he suspected him to be an insurgent, and that as soon as he was executed his ears should be cut off and his tongue cut out. On the following morning he invited three of his friends, brother officers, to breakfast, and presented to them, as a choice dish, the ears and tongue of the insurgent, cooked. His friends were horrified and reported it to the commanding officer. The cannibal was tried and condemned to death ; but he was subsequently pardoned by special order of the King of Spain, who was thoroughly cognizant of the circumstances of the case, and restored to his command.

The last riot of the Volunteers of Havana, on the 26th and 27th of November last, and which resulted in the shooting of eight young students of the medical school, and the condemnation to the chain-gang of thirty-two others, for the supposed profanation of the grave of a volunteer, is too fresh in the memory of everybody, to require our citing it as a proof of the impotence of the authorities and of the omnipotence of the prætorians. We merely wish to mention the fact that during the sitting of the court martial, Generals Venene and Clavigo, (the latter Sub-Inspector General of these very Volunteers,) and the Civil Governor of Havana, Lopez Rob-'erts, whom they insulted and assaulted, and whom they stigmatized as a thief, were kept imprisoned in the jail, as safe hostages that the heads of the students be delivered to them. The degradation of the Provisional Captain-General Crespò,' is also patent. Not satisfied with having been a docile tool in the hands of the Volunteers, he proved himself the most subservient to their interests, by forwarding to the Government of Madrid an incorrect statement of the disgraceful affair. This we deduce from the declarations made by the Government, who make it appear that the students had invaded the cemetery of Havana, for the purpose of exhuming the corpse of Castañon, whilst it is well known that all they did was to scratch the glass which covers the marble at the end of the niche.

All this however failed to satisfy the Volunteers, who expected probably another hecatomb with which to quench their thirst of blood ; and Count Valmaseda who, according to appearances is already beginning to lose his popularity among them, wished doubtless to reconquer their good graces by further proof of his illimitable desire to gratify them ; this is the meaning of the recent proclamation dated 27th of December. It seemed almost impossible, that, after his celebrated one of April 4, 1869, which Mr. Fish stigmatized as infamous, anything more barbarous could happen for the depopulation of a country; but the new proclamation proves that something was still wanting to perfect the work of destruction, and if the Duke of Alba, the relentless exterminator of the Low Countries, were alive, he would be justly jealous of Count Valmaseda, for having eclipsed his hitherto unparalleled glory as an executioner.

The proclamation of 1869 ordained that every male inhabitant over fifteen years of age found out of his house without justifiable reason should be shot ; that every house not occupied by Spanish troops, or over which a white flag was not hoisted, should be burned ; and that every woman living in the county in the jurisdictions of Bayamo and Jiguani should be brought into the cities, willingly or by force. The proclamation of December, 1871, ordains that all insurgent prisoners be shot; it condemns all who surrender, to the chain-gang; it orders that all white women found in the rural districts be exiled from the island, and that all the negro women taken under similar circumstances be delivered up to their owners, and that the latter be obliged to make them carry chains for four years. The proclamation places free women of color found in the country, in the same category as white women, but as they will, of course, be unable to prove the fact of their being free, they will either be sold as slaves for the benefit of the State, or some employee, either military or volunteer, will reap the benefit of their services, which is much more likely. However, Valmaseda's last proclamation has only publicly proclaimed the right to do what has been done since the commencement of the war ; the Spanish troops have never given quarter to their prisoners ; the volunteers have always shot all who fall into their hands ; and the women and children who have not been the victims either of the one or the other, are living on charity in the towns, or have been banished to foreign countries.

We have purposely avoided quoting the outrages which have been committed against the persons and property of American citizens, for they have been so numerous and they must be so vividly present to the people of the United States, that we have thought it unnecessary to remind them that their Government has not yet exacted just reparation for them. Their Government must understand the necessity of protecting those who still reside in Cuba from the consequences of the corruption and anarchy which obtain there.

Nor are this corruption and this anarchy confined to the Island of Cuba, they extend to Spain also. They penetrate into every artery of the nation, and even influence the resolutions of the Congress and the international relations of the Government.

Thus, it is, that we find a nation, already depleted both of people and resources, submitting in silence to an annual draft of twenty thousand of its sons, very few of whom are fated ever to return to their native land, for the purpose of sustaining a war waged against every principle of liberty and of justice.

Thus it is that, while in Cuba we find an unbridled militia, whose only law is rapine, whose only principle is the preservation of slavery, whose only instinct is the shedding of blood, placing and displacing governors and captains-general at its will; arresting, exiling, and murdering peaceful inhabitants, Spaniards and foreigners without distinction, in order to possess itself of their property; openly forming associations for the rewarding of assassins, deriding the tribunals of the nation, and rewarding calumniators who have been punished by them; in Spain, we find the tribunals and the supreme Government submitting resignedly to these misdeeds, and even sanctioning and approving them so far, that one colonial min- ister (Mr. Lopez de Ayala), accepted, as an honor, the uniform of a volunteer, at the very time that the other ministers, his colleagues, were the recipients of the grossest insults. What can men of this stamp in power care if their delegates do dis- obey their orders, if they do run their pen through a safe-con- duct to which the honor of the nation was pledged, or if they do shoot a dupe who, unfortunately, risked his life under the shield of Spanish loyalty?

Under the pressure of the opinion of the whole civilized world, and still more, perhaps, for the purpose of smoothing over the slight offered to the United States in declining the

4

good offices tendered for the termination of the Cuban conflict, the Government and Congress of Spain patched up a
burlesque of a law for the abolition of slavery, by which those
slaves only would be free who were still unborn, and those
who were on the brink of the grave ; but this law, farcical as
it was, alarmed the Spanish slaveholders of Cuba, and their
janizaries the volunteers, and this was enough to make a
dead letter of the law; nor did either the government or the
legislature ever dare to attempt its enforcement. For what
every body in Cuba knows full well, what the Spanish press
has published, and what has even been declared in the Spanish Congress, must be stated here ; those who, in union with
the government employees, fatten on the spoils of the country,
and who maintain the *statu quo* and the reign of terror in
Cuba, are principally the traders in, and the holders of negroes.
These men have ever been bitterly opposed to every political
reform and to the slightest modification of the system of slavery, fearful lest the door be opened for the destruction of
their cherished institution, to which they are indebted for
their ill-gotten wealth. The volunteers, under the plea of
patriotism, serve as tools in the hands of the slave-traders,
with the two-fold object of oppressing and plundering the
Cubans, and of preventing every attempt at abolition. They
frighten the government of Spain, and are enabled, by means
of their relations with old companions in Madrid, who grew
rich in Cuba, and above all, by the free expenditure of their
own means, to exercise an influence perfectly irresistible. To
this is to be attributed the fact, that the Spanish government,
in spite of the proverbial haughtiness of the nation, has tamely
allowed the United States to reproach them to their face
with having violated their promises voluntarily given, that
they would inaugurate measures for the abolition of slavery in Cuba. (See letter from Mr. Fish to Gen. Sickles, June
20, 1870). Abolition of slavery is not to be dreamed of as
long as there are Spaniards, and much less as long as there
are volunteers, on the island.

The Spanish Congress bows to this double pressure of the
volunteers and the slave-traders, and listens with magnani-
mous shamelessness to the insults of the latter, and to their

declaration that any laws which do not flatter their instincts will be repelled by them by force. To this same pressure is due the tone of each and every of the cabinets which succeed each other in Spain with the rapidity of the kaleidoscope ; not, one of them is ashamed of the war which is being waged in Cuba; all of them promise to continue it until the Cubans are exterminated. If any one of them ventures, though for the purpose of deception, to propose any compromise, although the compromise be rejected, the fact of its having been proposed is no sooner bruited about Madrid, than the head of the cabinet tragically disappears from the scene. Later on, his colleagues smite their breasts in Congress, and to avoid being considered traitors, deny their own acts, and the assasination of General Prim is buried in oblivion.

So thoroughly convinced is the Spanish Government of its inability to cope with the volunteers, that it has been obliged to swallow in silence the following words pronounced by Senator Mendez Vigo in the session of the 12th of July, 1871 : " There are people in Spain who propose to disarm the volunteers. Who can disarm them ? The Government? Will it attempt the task ? Has it the right or the force to do it ? The volunteers will not deliver up their arms." The Colonial Minister, interrupting him, said, " They will obey the Government." Senator Mendez Vigo replied, " They will not deliver up their arms *unless they receive positive guarantees.*"

The Minister of State said, " This is the exciting a rebellion." But Mr. Mendez closed his mouth by his reply : " The exciting to rebellion comes, Mr. Minister of State, from elsewhere." Here we see the volunteers, after insulting Congress for " *its abject degradation,*" accusing the Government in the Senate of provoking them to rebellion, and demanding from it positive guarantees before they lay down their arms.

Possibly one of these guarantees (and this completes and illumines the picture of Spanish anarchy in Cuba, and shows how impotent the Madrid government is to suppress it), may have been believed to be the late creation of a special order or decoration wherewith to reward the deserts and services of the volunteers in Cuba. The King of that *honorable* Spain has hereby thrown his cloak of ermine over the atrocities which have been, and which are still being perpetrated in Cuba ; and as if this did not suffice to assure the volunteers how thoroughly he accepts their acts, on the very day on which the civilized world was horrified at the slaughter of the 27th of November, this son of the *Re Galantuomo*, sends his thanks to the murderers "*for having preserved order in Havana*," and ordains that the breast of each of the thirty-two volunteers, who executed the eight innocent students, should be decorated with the " Cross of Cuba."

VII.

CONCLUSION.

A nation that fails to comply with its most solemn international obligations:

A nation which, in spite of these obligations and of the condemnation of the whole civilized world, continued for half a century trading in human flesh, and while apparently passing a law for abolition, obstinately maintains slavery:

A nation that, not satisfied with having tyrannized for more than three centuries over a cultivated people, wages a war of extermination against it because they rose for its liberty and independence, and that, finding itself unable with all its power to annihilate it by every method tolerated in wars between civilized nations, abdicates its sovereignty to a horde of merciless savages who disobey its laws, insult its legislatures, threaten its government with rebellion, and acknowledge the monarch only when he absolves and rewards their outrages against humanity and civilization:

Does such a nation deserve a place among the enlightened ones of the earth?

Is it true to say that it still governs in Cuba, simply because it still holds it in that same vulture's claw, which has mangled the heart of America?

Is it right that the republic of the United States should clasp the bloody hand of such a nation, as it would that of an honorable friend; or that it consent to its admission to a companionship with other American powers begotten from the liberties which the United States taught them?

And, a people who, wearied out by oppression, without

hope of reform or of any alleviation of its sufferings, stimulated by the liberty and the happiness of its great republican neighbor, determined to break its chains, even if all its wealth be consumed in the task of its regeneration :

A people whose first act on raising the cry of Independence, was to proclaim the emancipation of every slave, and the equality before the law of every race :

A people, who for more than three years, has sustained a war of devastation against a nation of tigers, with scarcely any weapons but their naked arms, and no aid but their own courage, without ever once losing faith in the righteousness of their cause, or in the certainty of its final triumph :

This people, we ask, has it no claim on the sympathies of other American nations, who, more blessed than itself, have already shaken off European control ?

In the name of justice, in the name of humanity, is it not entitled to the intervention of some providential force to compel its adversary to humanize the war ?

Does it not deserve that at least the same rights be accorded to it, as to its enemy ?

Would it not be an act worthy of this great Union to extend the hand of friendship to this people who, following in its footsteps, aspires to a place among the free peoples of America ?